TSUNAMI

TRIUMPH

Front cover photo courtesy of Getty Images
Back cover photos, clockwise from top left, courtesy of AP/Wide World Photos, Landov,
AP/Wide World Photos

All interior photos courtesy of AP/Wide World Photos

Editorial credits (unless otherwise noted):
UPI – stories on pages 14 (2), 18, 22, 26, 28, 32, 36
KRT – story on page 24

Special thanks to David Perel for his creative input and initiative

Content packaged by Mojo Media, Inc.
Editor: Joe Funk
Creative Director: Jason Hinman
Assistant Editor: Matt Springer

This book is available in quantity at special discounts for your group or organization.
For further information, contact:

Triumph Books
601 S. LaSalle St.
Suite 500
Chicago, Illinois 60605
Phone: (312) 939-3330
Fax: (312) 663-3557

Printed in the United States of America

ASIAN DISASTER RELIEF
The Publisher will be donating 50% of all earnings generated by this book to Asian disaster
relief. QUEBECOR WORLD, the publication's printer, will also be donating a portion of its
earnings to the relief efforts.

Contents

Relief Organizations Working in the Disaster Area

HOW TO DONATE: Below is a list of charities providing assistance to people affected by the earthquake and tsunamis. You can donate money to them by mail, phone, or through their web sites, which are listed below.

Action Against Hunger
247 West 37th Street
New York, NY 10018
212-967-7800
www.actionagainsthunger.org

Adventist Development and Relief Agency
(ADRA) International
Asia Tsunami Crisis Fund
12501 Old Columbia Pike
Silver Spring, MD 20904
800-424-ADRA (2372)
www.adra.org

Air Serv International
6583 Merchant Place, Suite 100
Warrenton, VA 20187
540-428-2323
www.airserv.org

American Friends Service Committee
1501 Cherry Street
Philadelphia, PA 19102
888-588-2372
www.afsc.org

American Jewish World Service
45 W. 36th St., 10th Fl.
New York, NY 10018
212-736-2597
www.ajws.org

American Leprosy Missions
One ALM Way
Greenville, SC 29687
864-271-7040
www.leprosy.org

American Refugee Committee
Tsunami Relief
430 Oak Grove Street, Suite 204
Minneapolis, MN 55403
612-872-7060
www.archq.org

AmeriCares
88 Hamilton Ave
Stamford, CT 06902
800-486-4357
www.americares.org

Baptist World Aid
Asia Tidal Waves
405 North Washington Street
Falls Church, VA 22046
703 790 8980
www.bwanet.org/bwaid

Brother's Brother Foundation
1200 Galveston Ave
Pittsburgh, PA 15233
412-321-3160
www.brothersbrother.org

CARE
151 Ellis Street NE
Atlanta, GA 30303
800-521-CARE
www.careusa.org

Catholic Medical Mission Board
10 West 17th Street
New York, New York 10011
800-678-5659
www.cmmb.org

Catholic Relief Services
209 West Fayette Street
Baltimore, MD 21201
800-736-3467
www.catholicrelief.org

Christian Children's Fund
Child Alert Fund
PO Box 26484
Richmond, Virginia - 23261-6484
800-776-6767
www.ChristianChildrensFund.org

Christian Reformed World Relief Committee
(CRWRC)
South Asia Earthquake
2850 Kalamazoo Ave. SE
Grand Rapids, MI, 49560
800-55-CRWRC
www.crwrc.org

Church World Service
#6970 Southern Asia Earthquake PO Box
968
Elkhart, IN 46515
800-297-1516
www.churchworldservice.org

Convoy of Hope
330 S. Patterson Avenue
Springfield, MO 65802
417-823-8998
www.convoyofhope.org

Direct Relief International
27 South La Patera Lane
Santa Barbara, CA 93117
805-964-4767
www.directrelief.org

Doctors of the World-USA
375 West Broadway, 4th Floor
New York, NY 10012
212-226-9890
www.dowusa.org

Feed the Children, Inc. (FTC)
333 North Meridian Ave
Oklahoma City, OK 73107
405-942-0228
www.feedthechildren.org

Food for the Hungry, Inc.
Tsunami Relief
1224 E. Washington St.
Phoenix, AZ 85034
800-2-HUNGERS
www.fh.org

Geneva Global Inc
1550 Liberty Ridge Drive
Suite 330
Wayne, PA 19087
www.GenevaGlobal.com

Habitat for Humanity International
Asia Tsunami Response Fund
121 Habitat St
Americus, GA 31709
229-924-6935
www.habitat.org

Heart to Heart International
401 S. Clairborne
Suite 302
Olathe, KS 66062
888-800-4327
www.hearttoheart.org

Helen Keller International
352 Park Avenue South
Suite 1200
New York, NY 10010
877-KELLER4 (877-535-5374)
www.hki.org

HOPE Worldwide, Ltd.
353 West Lancaster Avenue
Wayne, PA 19087-3907
610-254-8800
www.hopeww.org

Interchurch Medical Assistance, Inc.
South Asia Tsunami Relief
P.O. Box 429
New Windsor, MD 21776
877-241-7952
www.interchurch.org

International Medical Corps
Tsunami Emergency Response
1919 Santa Monica Blvd., Suite 300
Santa Monica, CA 90404-1950
800-481-4462
www.imcworldwide.org

International Medical Services
for Health (INMED)
INMED Partnerships for Children
45449 Severn Way, Suite 161
Sterling, VA 20166
703-444-4477 x214
www.inmed.org

International Orthodox Christian
Charities (IOCC)
Asia Disaster Response
P.O. Box 630225
Baltimore, MD 21263-0225
877-803-4622
www.iocc.org

International Relief Teams
Asia Earthquake/Floods
3547 Camino Del Rio South, Suite C
San Diego, CA 92108
619-284-7979
www.IRTeams.org

International Rescue Committee
PO Box 5058
Hagerstown, MD 21741-9874
877-REFUGEE or 733-8433
www.theIRC.org

Jesuit Refugee Service/USA
1616 P Street NW
Suite 300
Washington, DC 20036
202-462-0400
www.jrsusa.org

Lutheran World Relief
South Asia Tsunami
700 Light Street
Baltimore, MD 21230
410-230-2700
www.lwr.org

MAP International
P.O. Box 215000
Brunswick, GA 31521
800-225-8550
www.map.org

Mercy Corps
Southeast Asia Earthquake
Dept. W
PO Box 2669
Portland, OR 97208-2669
800-852-2100
www.mercycorps.org

Mercy-USA for Aid and
Development
Tsunami Disaster Relief
44450 Pinetree Drive, Suite 201
Plymouth, Michigan 48170-3869
800-556-3729
www.mercyusa.org

Nazarene Compassionate
Ministries, Inc.
720 S. Rogers Rd, Suite A,
Olathe, KS 66062
1-800-214-4999
www.ncmi.org

Northwest Medical Teams
SE Asia Disaster Relief Fund
PO Box 10
Portland, OR 97207
800-959-4325 (HEAL)
www.nwmedicalteams.org

Operation Blessing International
Asia Earthquake
and Tsunami Relief
977 Centerville Turnpike
Virginia Beach, VA 23463
800-730-2537
www.ob.org

Operation USA
8320 Melrose Ave. #200
Los Angeles, CA 90069
800-678-7255
www.opusa.org

Oxfam America
Asian Earthquake Fund
PO Box 1211
Albert Lea, MN 56007-1211
800-77-OXFAM
www.oxfamamerica.org

Project HOPE
Asia Tsunami Response
255 Carter Hall Lane
Millwood, VA 22646
800-544-4673
www.projecthope.org

Red Cross (American Red Cross)
International Response Fund
P.O. BOX 37243
Washington, DC 20013
800-HELP-NOW
www.redcross.org

Refugees International
1705 N Street NW
Washington, DC 20036
202-828-0110
www.refugeesinternational.org

Relief International
Asia Earthquake Response
1575 Westwood Blvd., Suite 201
Los Angeles, CA 90024
800-573-3332
www.ri.org

Salvation Army World Service
Office (SAWSO)
South Asia Relief Fund
615 Slaters Lane
Alexandria, VA, 22313
800-SAL-ARMY
www.1800salarmy.org

Samaritan's Purse
P.O. Box 3000
Boone, NC 28607
Phone (828) 262-1980
Fax (828) 266-1053
www.samaritanspurse.org

Save the Children
54 Wilton Road
Westport, CT 06880
1-800-728-3843
www.savethechildren.org

Unitarian Universalist
Service Committee
UUSC-UUA Tsunami Relief
Fund
P.O. Box 845259
Boston, MA 02284-5259
617-868-6600
www.uusc.org

United Methodist
Committee on Relief
Advance #274305, South Asia
Emergency
475 Riverside Drive, Room 330
New York, NY 10115
212-870-3815
www.methodistrelief.org

United Way of America
United Way South
Asia Response Fund
P.O. Box 9193
Uniondale, NY 11555
703-519-0092
www.unitedway.org/tsunamire-
sponse

US Fund for UNICEF
Tsunami Relief Fund
333 E. 38th Street
New York, NY 10016
800-4-UNICEF
www.unicefusa.org

Vietnam Veterans of America
Foundation (VVAF)
1725 Eye Street NW, Suite 400
Washington, DC 20006
202-483-9222
www.vvaf.org

World Concern
Asia Earthquake and Tsunami
19303 Fremont Avenue North
Seattle, WA 98133
800-755-5022
www.worldconcern.org

World Hope International
Asia Relief
P.O. Box 96338
Washington DC 20090
888-466-4673
www.worldhope.org

World Relief
SE Asia Earthquake/Tsunamis
7 East Baltimore St
Baltimore MD 21202
800-535-5433
www.worldrelief.org

World Vision
P.O. Box 70288
Tacoma, WA 98481-0288
888-56-CHILD
www.worldvision.org

Information courtesy of USAID,
which is a U.S. government
agency responsible for economic
and humanitarian assistance
around the world. USAID
works together with many of the
organizations above to provide
assistance to the victims of the
earthquake/tsunami. You may
choose to contribute to any of the
relief agencies above, all of which
are working with contributions
from the general public.

Introduction

On Dec. 26, 2004, the earth beneath the Indian Ocean opened virtually without warning and changed the lives of millions of people across the globe. The enormous earthquake and subsequent tsunamis claimed literally countless lives from the southern Asian coastlines of numerous countries, leaving in its wake a trail of devastation and despair.

Tens of thousands of children were among the dead, and thousands upon thousands more were left parentless, homeless, and seemingly hopeless. Families in the farthest reaches of the globe were ripped apart, and economies throughout the affected region have been crushed with the same force as everything else that stood in the path of the killer waves.

In the days and weeks afterward, however, as incredible tales of survival, heartwarming stories of families

Flowers are left on a beach at Khoa Lak, Thailand, during a ceremony for the tsunami victims.

reuniting, and unprecedented acts of heroism and generosity emerged through the rubble, we as a people began to feel a renewed sense of faith and hope. For a moment in time, it seemed, enemies put their differences aside and the world came together as one.

This publication was conceived to celebrate the heroes, to salute and aid the survivors, to honor the victims, and to perpetuate that ray of hope that has been spawned by this world-changing event.

From the Publishers

Indonesians prepare to leave with a boat full of relief goods to be taken to remote places, at a river in the center of Banda Aceh, Indonesia, Sunday Jan. 2, 2005.

Men walk by boats on the town's main road after a tidal wave hit the southern Sri Lankan town of Galle.

Rescue and clean-up crew survey a flooded lobby at the Seapearl Beach Hotel along Patong Beach on Phuket Island.

(top) Dec. 26, 2004 at 10:20 a.m. local time, slightly less than four hours after the 6:28 a.m. (local Sri Lanka time) earthquake and shortly after the moment of tsunami impact. (above) This is a natural color satellite image showing the coastline on the southwestern city of Kalutara, Sri Lanka taken Jan. 1, 2005.

Part I

SURVIVING AGAINST ALL ODDS

Jan. 5, 2005. Seventeen U.S. Marines arrive in the Sri Lankan capital Colombo with two helicopters and an additional staff of 30 U.S. Air Force military communication and technical experts who will serve as the helicopter ground crew. They will take part in the aid, rescue and recovery mission going on in the region in response to the devastating tsunami.

Python saves 9-year-old twins

BANDA ACEH, Indonesia,

A python saved the lives of an Indonesian woman and twin girls as they were being swept away in the deadly tsunami. A 26-year-old clothing vendor identified only as Riza said she was swept away when the tsunami hit Banda Aceh. As she was drifting in the water, she saw her badly injured neighbor and her 9-year-old twin daughters also caught in the current.

"The mother shouted, 'Please help save my children. Let me be, but please save my children,' " Riza said.

As she struggled for her own life and that of the twins, Riza said a large snake as long as a telephone pole approached her. She and the nine-year-olds rested on the reptile, which was drifting along with the current.

"Thank God, we landed on higher ground where the water level was only about a meter deep. The twins, who were badly injured, were safe."

Riza said she slapped her face to make sure she wasn't dreaming, then realized, "God still loves me." ■

Man survives two weeks at sea

JAKARTA

An Indonesian man swept to sea by the tsunami was recovering after surviving two weeks adrift on debris. Ari Afrizal, 21, was building a house with friends in the northern Aceh town of Calang when the tsunami struck Dec. 26. He was first pushed inland and then sucked out to sea when the waters receded.

He said for the first 24 hours, he clung to a log, but then spotted a damaged wooden fishing boat and moved into it. Unsure how long it would remain afloat, he began collecting debris and created a raft on which he lived, eating floating coconuts.

"I managed to survive as I ate the flesh of old coconuts for about 12 days. For three days I didn't get to eat anything," he said. "I gave up all hope of living. The first day I clung to a piece of wood, the second day I retrieved a small fishing boat but it was leaking. I was in the small boat for four days before I managed to get on a raft."

Afrizal said he waved repeatedly at passing ships, but none stopped for him until Sunday when the UAE-registered al-Yamamah appeared on the horizon.

"I managed to whistle at the ship and then waved my hands. The ship sped on but it sounded the klaxon and I stood up. I thought the ship had left the area and I sat down and cried. But the ship returned and cheered me up," he said.

"I then waved at them as I knew I was safe."

Ari is the third tsunami survivor to be rescued at sea. A Japanese cargo boat rescued an Indonesian from the Indian Ocean eight days after the 23-year-old was swept away by the tsunami.

U.S. Navy helicopter crew from USS Abraham Lincoln unload fresh water cans to tsunami victims amid the ruins of their village on the western coast of Aceh province, Indonesia. United States military said that they would reopen an airport on nearby Sabang island to relieve the pressure on Banda Aceh during the relief operation.

Rizal Shahputra said he managed to stay afloat by clinging to driftwood. He survived on rainwater and coconuts, which he pried open with a door latch, while scores of others died around him. Shahputra was cleaning a mosque in Banda Aceh on Sumatra Island when the tsunami struck.

He was pulled from the sea by the cargo ship MV Durban Bridge and brought to the port of Klang in Malaysia. He said he clung to floating planks with scores of other people—all of whom were eventually swallowed up by the sea.

Shahputra's survival was similar to that of an Indonesian woman who held on to a sago palm tree for five days in the Indian Ocean. Malawati, 23, was rescued by a Malaysian tuna ship. ▪

(above) Three-year-old Sundari, who survived the tsunami, sits on her father's boat with her pet cat, at Srinavasapuri in Madras, India. She lost her brother and some of her relatives are still missing. (right) Survivors arrive on a boat from far-flung areas at Banda Aceh Tuesday Jan. 11, 2005, more than two weeks after a devastating tsunami ravaged the capital and other coastal towns in northwest Indonesia.

Tourist uses towels to save family from wave

Umberto Giovi, 42, from Rio Elba, Italy, with his Thai girlfriend Isari Chanswan, left, and Anucha Jangho, a restaurant staff member, hold a banner they made to signal rescue flights that they were alive after the tsunami.

LONDON

A British tourist saved his wife and children from the Asian tsunami by tying them to the top of a palm tree with towels. Stephen Boulton detailed his desperate ploy as the first dedicated emergency flight from the disaster zone arrived at London's Heathrow Airport. Boulton was celebrating his 34th birthday with his wife and three children in the Maldives when the tidal wave struck, driving him to lead his family through strong currents and up the tree.

"I strapped them to the branches with the four towels," Boulton said. "Suddenly it was like someone had pulled a plug and the tide just swept out back into the ocean carrying everything, people, sun beds, bunga-lows. It was awful."

Boulton was among 94 people aboard the British Airways Boeing 747, chartered by the Foreign Office.

Another passenger on the flight was Charlie Anderson of London, who was snorkeling with his girlfriend off the Thai coast when the first of three waves struck and sucked him into turbulent water.

"The next thing I knew I was washed up on a beach, said Anderson, 28. "Bodies were floating in the water and it was five or six hours before I saw my girlfriend again." ■

A volunteer fumigates inside a mosque used as a refugee camp Thursday, Jan. 13, 2005 in Banda Aceh, Indonesia. As the threat of cholera diminished by the day because clean water is increasingly getting to tsunami survivors, the danger of malaria and dengue fever epidemics is now beginning to skyrocket, experts say.

Survivors of the Tsunami use an elephant to pull a vehicle from the destroyed village of Lam Jamek, Banda Aceh, Sumatra, Indonesia.

Man buried for 13 days

GALLE, Sri Lanka

A man found Saturday trapped under tsunami-created rubble has been rushed to a hospital in Galle, Sri Lanka. The man was trapped under the rubble during the Dec. 26 tsunami. He remained trapped for 13 days. Doctors at Karapitiya Hospital said he was suffering from pneumonia and severe dehydration, but he will certainly live.

"Miracles do happen," said Dr. Chandra Pala Mudanngake. ■

(above) Tidal wave survivors walk past an image of Buddha amid the rubble in the destroyed downtown area of Galle in southern Sri Lanka. Legs folded, smiling serenely, several Buddha statues of cement and plaster sit unscathed amid collapsed brick walls and other debris in the center of Galle, a southern town devastated by the tsunami onslaught. To many residents, the survival of the statues is a divine sign. (right) Todd Yetman, of Toronto, Canada, who is on his honeymoon, looks at a damaged ship washed up on Patong Beach.

A man puts rubble on a fire while cleaning his home in Banda Aceh, Sumatra island, Indonesia, Wednesday, Jan. 12.

Girl's attention in class proves to be a life-saver

(above) A survivor searches for her missing relatives amidst the rubble at Banda Aceh Tuesday Jan. 11, 2005. (right) Thai muslims pose for photos near a beached police boat at the site of the tsunami devastation in Khao Lak in southern Thailand.

Weather-alert machines are good, and forecasters are, well, usually reliable, but in some cases, your own eyes and brain aren't bad either. Tilly Smith, a 10-year-old British girl vacationing with her family on a Thai island, recognized the signs of an impending tsunami from her geography class. Watching the abrupt withdrawal of the tide and small bubbles forming on the beach, she recalled her teacher saying there was about 10 minutes between the time the ocean recedes and the moment a tsunami strikes.

Tilly immediately alerted her mother; the beach and a neighboring hotel were hastily evacuated, perhaps saving hundreds of lives. ■

Man survives 11-day burial under house

JAKARTA, Jan. 8

A 70-year-old man survived 11 days buried under the remains of his house in Indonesia's Aceh province. Muhammad Zaini, a father of six, was discovered by relief workers searching the rubble in the Puta Alam neighborhood of Banda Aceh. He was in weak condition and rushed to a military hospital.

"The soil was shaking, the house's walls were collapsed. It's likely that I was floating on water and carried away before the falling wall hit on me. I'm squeezed," Zaini said.

"Since then, I did not remember what happen and how I could survive. I only drink water that existed around me, because I can't move to anywhere."

Zaini said he was alone in the house when the tsunami hit. He said that he was unconscious at times and had dreams of birds bringing him food.

"As a matter of fact, maybe I am already dead," Zaini muttered.

Wild animals escape waves. ■

An American Navy flight crewman carries a young injured evacuee Monday, Jan 3, 2005 at the airport.

Thai workers try to capture an Indo-Pacific humpback dolphin in a lagoon in Khao Lak in southern Thailand on Wednesday, Jan. 5, 2005. Rescue workers freed the dolphin from the small lagoon where the tsunami had dumped it, returning it to the Andaman Sea in a rare story of survival 10 days after the massive waves crushed posh tourist resorts in the surrounding area.

Amazing Animals

COLOMBO, Sri Lanka

While the tsunami death toll in Sri Lanka continued to soar, officials said wild animals seemed to have escaped the disaster, with no dead animals found. Tsunami waves reached two miles inland to the island's biggest wildlife reserve, home to elephants, deer, jackals and crocodiles. Many tourists drowned but, to the surprise of wildlife officials, apparently none of the animals died.

Debbie Marter, who works on a wild tiger conservation program on the Indonesian island of Sumatra, one of the worst-hit areas in the disaster, said the news did not surprise her. "Wild animals in particular are extremely sensitive," she said. "They've got extremely good hearing and they will probably have heard this flood coming into the distance.

The evidence highlights claims that animals may possess a sixth sense that alerts them to impending danger. The current reports may add to the understanding of animal behavior and possibly be of use in the future as an early warning system for humans. ▪

A villager cleans debris following Tsunami Tidal wave, triggered by Indonesia's huge earthquake, that hit a village in Penang Island, northwestern Malaysia, Tuesday, Dec. 28, 2004.

Indonesian tsunami victims wait to be evacuated by Indonesian amphibious navy vessels in the destroyed town of Calang, 40 miles south west of Banda Aceh in the province of Aceh.

An Indonesian navy ship is seen along the coast of Calang, north of Meulaboh, on Sumatra's western coast.

Underwater couple survives tsunami

Rescuers look for survivors at Yala Reserve Wildlife Park. Wild life officials expressed surprise Wednesday that they found no evidence of large-scale animal deaths from the weekend's massive tsunami, indicating that animals may have sensed the wave coming and fled to higher ground.

OAKLAND, Calif.

A California couple scuba diving off Thailand were unaware strange water movements they felt was the deadly tsunami passing over them. In e-mailed messages to her mother in Oakland, Faye Wachs told how she and her husband were underwater off Ko Phi Phi Island in Thailand when they noticed the water visibility worsen, and felt as if they were being sucked downward.

As they surfaced, Wachs said they noticed a lot of trash, and then increasingly large pieces of debris, and assumed a boat had gone down. Then they began seeing bodies.

Helen Wachs said her daughter didn't know what had happened until the dive master got a text message from his wife telling him about the catastrophe.

Wachs told her mother the couple "lost everything but our lives," as their beach hotel was no longer there. The couple was due to arrive home shortly, after which Wachs told her mother they would need "some serious counseling." ■

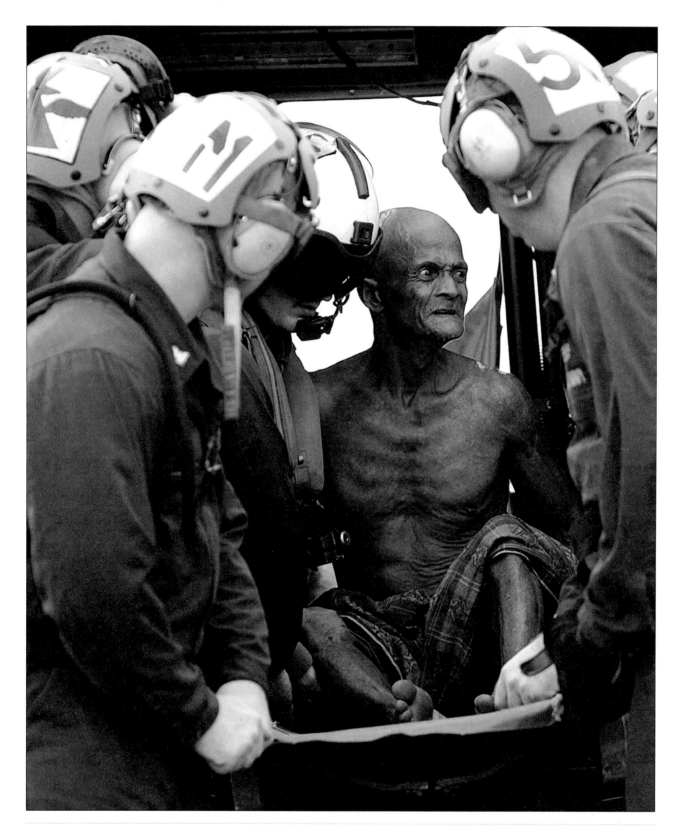

American Navy flight crewmen carry an injured evacuee Monday, Jan 3, 2005 at the airport in Banda Aceh, the capital of Aceh province in northwestern Indonesia.

An aerial view of Pattinapakam, a slum which was destroyed by a tsunami, near Madras, India.

A survivor of the tsunami use an elephant to remove rubble from the destroyed village of Lam Jamek.

Tsunami victims from Hut Bay stand next to the word HELP written on the ground seeking attention, in India's Andaman and Nicobar archipelago.

Swedish toddler reunited with father

PHUKET, Thailand

A 20-month-old Swedish boy, separated from his parents by the tsunami in Thailand, has been reunited with his father. Hannes Bergstrom was found alone on a roadside near a Thai beach resort and he was taken by helicopter to a hospital for treatment. The hospital staff posted his photo on the Internet in an effort to locate his family.

His uncle, who spotted the photo, claimed the boy and set up the reunion with the father. Hannes' father, Marko Bergstrom, and grandfather, Asko, are also recovering in the hospital. But Hannes' mother, Susanne, has not yet been found. His face scratched and pocked with mosquito bites and his hand band-aged, Hannes looked bemused as his father choked up with emotion. The father, also scratched and bruised, lay in his hospital bed, holding Hannes with balloons around them.

There were reports that a Thai princess arranged the helicopter that carried the child from the roadside to the hospital. Bergstrom said he had been told of the reports.

"I have been to Thailand seven times, and this time only confirmed what I know about Thai people—that they are so generous and caring, he said. "She has saved his life, but also my soul because I couldn't survive if I lost them both." ∎

In these photos released by Durban Bridge, tsunami survivor Acehnese Rizal Shahputra stands on the tree branches and waves to a cargo ship after being spotted by the crew of a container vessel in the Indian Ocean, 100 nautical miles from the shores of Aceh province Monday, Jan. 3, 2005. The Indonesian man swept off shore by the tsunami was found afloat on tree branches and debris, the second person to be found alive at sea by Malaysian ships days after the disaster.

(above) A Sentinel tribal man aims with his bow and arrow at an Indian Coast Guard helicopter as it flies over their island for survey in Indias Andaman and Nicobar archipelago, Tuesday, Dec, 28, 2004. From circumstantial evidence, officials say fate and the ancient knowledge of secret signals in the wind and sea have combined to save the five indigenous tribes living for centuries in the southern archipelago of Andaman and Nicobar from the catastrophic tsunami that lashed Asian coastlines last week. But the fate of the tribes – on the verge of extinction – will be known with certainty only after officials complete a survey of their remote islands. (right) Local villagers use a makeshift raft to cross a river where a bridge destroyed by the tsunamis once stood. The only road linking coastal cities on Sumatra was turned into an obstacle course by the tsunami, complicating aid deliveries and turning what was a five-hour journey into a many day trek for victims of the disaster.

HELP & HOPE

Indian army soldiers unload drinking water and other relief materials supplied by the government of India, for tsunami victims in Car Nicobar, in India's southeastern Andaman. Twelve of the 15 villages of Car Nicobar, one of the most secluded of the Andaman and Nicobar islands in the Bay of Bengal, were flattened under the Dec. 26, 2004 tsunami that ravaged 4.5 miles of the island in its first sweep.

Marines arrive in Sri Lanka to deliver tsunami aid By Lennox Samuels

The Dallas Morning News
COLOMBO, Sri Lanka

The Marines have landed. An advance contingent of U.S. Marines arrived at Colombo's airport, along with U.S. Air Force communications and technical experts.

Eventually about 1,500 U.S. troops are expected to be deployed around Sri Lanka, where the Dec. 26 tsunami killed more than 30,000 people and displaced 850,000 more.

U.S. Embassy spokesman Chris Long stressed that the troops would be used only for humanitarian work. They are expected to help repair roads and bridges. Tsunami damage has hampered access to some stricken areas.

U.N. officials said the Marines brought heavy-lifting helicopters, bulldozers and generators, along with tons of food, water and medical supplies.

American forces have already been on the ground for several days in Indonesia, using helicopters to deliver desperately needed food and relief supplies and rescuing scores of people left injured, hungry and weak by the tsunamis there.

Secretary of State Colin Powell—himself a battle-hardened military veteran—flew over the devastation on the island of Sumatra and said he was shocked by the destruction.

"I've been in war, and I've have been through a number of hurricanes, tornadoes and other relief operations, but I have never seen anything like this," the retired general said.

"I cannot begin to imagine the horror that went through the families and all of the people who heard this noise coming and then had their lives snuffed out by this wave. The power of the wave to destroy bridges, to destroy factories, to destroy homes, to destroy crops, to destroy everything in its path is amazing."

Workers broke ground for four refugee camps on Sumatra, where an estimated 1 million are homeless.

Powell will attend a summit in the Indonesian capital, Jakarta, where world leaders will discuss how to best distribute aid to victims of the Dec. 26 earthquake and tsunamis.

New pledges of aid continue to come. Australia announced a package of $764 million in grants and loans, making it the No. 1 single donor so far. Germany pledged $674 million. Earlier, Japan promised $500 million.

In New York, the U.N.'s emergency relief coordinator, Jan Egeland, said total pledges from donor governments had grown to between $3 billion and $4 billion, an amount he described as "just incredible."

Egeland also praised the United States for help he said only America could have delivered.

Egeland said the United Nations has now set up operations centers in Sri Lanka, Indonesia and other affected countries and asked that the world body be allowed to carry out its work in a coordinated manner.

U.N. officials raised their estimate of the regional death toll to 156,000 people—50,000 of them children—in 11 countries. They added that an additional 1 million children were at risk of contracting disease or being victimized by people traffickers or pedophiles. The confirmed death toll was more than

The United States Navy carrier USS Abraham Lincoln hauls relief supplies to survivors of the tsunami disaster.

139,000.

In Sri Lanka, UNICEF executive director Carol Bellamy visited areas hardest hit by the tsunami and met with government, rebel and non-governmental officials.

"I am aware that there are parts of the country that have not yet been reached by relief workers and that the suffering among the survivors there is severe," she said.

Indeed, heavy rains slowed relief operations in some areas of Sri Lanka that sustained the greatest damage. A number of Sri Lankan military helicopters that had been airlifting food in eastern Ampara district, where more than 10,000 people lost their lives, were grounded by rains.

In much of the region, this is the start of the mon-

Acehnese residents struggle to board a Malaysian Air Force Sea King helicopter to leave tsunami-ravaged town of Meulaboh, Aceh province.

soon season. Officials said the rains and flooding also raise fears of waterborne disease, especially among children.

World Food Program trucks fanned out across the country, delivering aid to needy and unruly crowds who scrambled for food supplies in such hard-hit areas as Ampara, Batticaloa, Trincomalee and Mullaitivu.

In camps for displaced persons, officials were trying to organize educational programs on sanitation, counseling sessions and social activities for children. A number of volunteers spent their time identifying children who had lost parents. ■

A young girl is amongst many other Hong Kong residents who donated money for tsunami victims at the Hong Kong Stadium, Saturday, Jan. 1, 2005, shortly before the start of a fund-raising show during which local celebrities and dignitaries as well as members of the general public donated money for relief operations in devastated southern Asia.

U.S. doctors offer tsunami aid By Dawn Fallik

Knight Ridder Newspapers

PHILADELPHIA

Dr. Fred Henretig wants to go to Indonesia. Or Sri Lanka. Or India. Anywhere the Children's Hospital of Philadelphia emergency doctor is needed. As worries increase about a wave of water-borne killers, such as cholera and dysentery, medical professionals nationwide are anxious to help. But like hundreds of doctors around the country, Henretig is in a holding pattern, waiting for the tsunami-hit countries to give the OK to come.

"It seems like the most compelling disaster that I've heard of in my lifetime," said Henretig, who also heads the Philadelphia Poison Control Center.

"There are sick and injured kids there, and I think it's going to get worse."

But even as doctors here are packing their bags, medical agencies in the tsunami-hit countries are telling U.S. officials to send money first and come later.

Although some agencies, such as Doctors Without Borders, have sent medical help, most of their physicians have come from nearby countries, agency officials said. They believe that U.S. healing hands will be needed in about a month, to help relieve those there.

Dr. Errol R. Alden, executive director for the American Academy of Pediatrics, based in Illinois, said they've had had several doctors call, trying to find a way to help.

But after contacting several pediatric hospitals in Sri Lanka, Thailand, and India, the word came back that it was financial, not human, help that was immediately needed.

"They basically said 'Please don't send people right away,'" said Alden. "It's really best to have people who are trained there, and are culturally sensitive provide services first."

Right now, the agencies are asking for vaccinations and money to help them buy supplies, he said. The most pressing need is to stop diseases like cholera and dysentery, which are caused by contaminated water and food, doctors said.

The diseases cause massive diarrhea, and the worry is that thousands of children will die from dehydration. But basic preventative skills and treatment, such as serving safe water, can be taught by non-doctors, said Alden.

Dr. David Jaslow, chief of Emergency Medical Services at Albert Einstein Healthcare Network in Philadelphia, has responded to hurricanes in Florida and specializes in domestic search and rescue missions.

Visitors need shelter and food and clean water, and there's precious little supplies available.

Dr. Eardley Wickramasinghe, a family practitioner at St. Vincent Health Center in Erie, Pa., had planned to leave for Sri Lanka on Dec. 28. He originally hoped to visit family back home and attend the Asian American International Medical Conference—coincidentally scheduled in Sri Lanka starting on Jan. 2.

After the tsunami hit, the doctor prepared to visit as planned, armed with supplies and planning on helping. Instead he was asked to wait.

"We were planning to go, but I talked to folks in Sri Lanka and they wanted us to work from here to fund raise for material and medicines to be shipped," said Dr. Wickramasinghe. "There were quite a few of the doc-

Tennis star Venus Williams eyes the ball before returning to Russian opponent Vera Zvonareva on the second day of the Watsons Water Championships Challenge 2005 women's tennis exhibition tournament at Hong Kong's Victoria Park. According to organizers $64,000 will be donated from the tournament's ticket sales to victims of the earthquake and tsunami disaster.

tors from the conference already there, so they had a lot of people already."

Wickramasinghe said he hopes to still go to help _ but maybe in another month of so.

In the meantime, Henretig, of CHOP, said he will be patient and wait until he can pack his black bag and go.

"What I'm waiting for is some sort of set-up where you can get off the plane and take a taxi and report for work in some clinic, and they say 'Here, you take care of these kids,'" he said. "So far, everyone is sitting tight and hoping to hear." ■

A U.S. Navy Seahawk helicopter flies an emergency relief mission over tsunami devastated Aceh province, Indonesia, on Jan. 2, 2005. They may not have been endowed with sleek, space age lines, but between them the Hercules and the Seahawk are proving the stars of the aerial relief operation in Indonesia.

The French flag is brought to half staff by two Republican Guards at the presidential Elysee Palace in Paris Monday, Jan. 3, 2005, in honor of the victims of the tidal wave.

Tsunami survivors rely on faith, helping others to ease their pain By Ben Stocking

Knight Ridder Newspapers
BANDA ACEH, Indonesia

Nearly two weeks after a tsunami and earthquake razed the northwestern shore of Sumatra, many survivors remain terrified by aftershocks, stunned by deaths, and, in many cases, hungry.

But they don't complain. Even those with ghastly injuries and staggering losses suffer with dignity and unshaken faith.

Like Teuku Zahria, who lost his brother and his home, survivors sustained themselves by helping others and praying to Allah. "I cried for three days after the tsunami came," said Zahria, 55. "Then I decided it is better to pitch in than to cry."

He found an unusual way to ease his pain: pulling dead bodies from the endless muck and debris left by the tsunami.

A devout Muslim, he considered this his duty to his community and the dead.

"If something happens to our brothers and sisters, we must help them," Zahria said as he wrapped three bodies in plastic sheets and placed them by the side of the road outside Banda Aceh, the provincial capital.

He estimated that he had recovered 200 bodies this week.

He wore plastic flip-flops and did his work without gloves. His feet and hands were covered with black grime from rummaging around in the endless mud and debris.

"We can't run away from people who need us," Zahria said.

There is so much need, so much loss. Much like after

Villagers affected by the tsunami line up for relief materials unloaded from a truck near the harbor area in Nagappattinam in the southern Indian state of Tamil Nadu.

the Sept. 11, 2001, attacks in New York, signs have sprung up around Banda Aceh with pictures of the missing. One showed two men who were last seen enjoying a game of golf by the sea.

Chairul, a 4-year-old-girl, and Ainul, her 7-year-old

This photo released by the White House shows former Presidents Bush, left, and Bill Clinton filming a public service announcement encouraging the American people to make cash donations to the tsunami relief effort through www.usafreedomcorps.gov.

南亞地震海嘯救援工作

Pay　聯合國兒童基金會 UNICEF

Date 29/12/2004

or bearer

HK Dollar　港幣伍拾萬元正

HK$500,000

brother, watched the tsunami suck their parents out to sea.

Chairul began life as an orphan buried to her neck in sand. Ainul began his stuck in the top of a palm tree. That's where the tsunami left them.

Now they live in a refugee camp. They keep asking when their mother and father will return.

But the survivors in the camp, each with a terrible story to tell, aren't bitter, said Nahabani, 52.

As with some other refugees, Nahabani's house survived. He came to the camp because there were too many corpses in his neighborhood and he was afraid of being alone.

The camp is just a cluster of tents on the side of a hill on the outskirts of Banda Aceh, but it's high enough to be spared from a tsunami.

When aftershocks come, refugees scream and run uphill, convinced that another tsunami will follow.

Almost all are Muslims; women wear headscarves, men wear skullcaps.

The earthquake and tsunami have deepened their belief in Allah.

"God is trying to test us," said Nahabani, who like many here goes by one name. "We must get closer to

Hong Kong action star Jackie Chan presents a check for $64,000 to United Nations Children's Fund representative. Chan donated the money to UNICEF's earthquake and tsunami relief efforts in south Asia.

him. We must be strong. We must pray more. We must read the Quran more."

Before the tsunami, Nahabani prayed five times a day, as is mandatory for Muslims here in the Sunni region of Aceh.

Now, he kneels to pray 10 times a day.

Dedi, 21, offered a penitent's explanation for the disaster as he sifted through the rubble of his home: "God is angry," he said. "He can make the whole world drown."

Dedi's mother died in the tsunami, and he was trying to recover some of her jewelry. He found nothing.

"This probably happened because the Achenese people made some mistakes that made God angry," Dedi said. "But it is impossible to be angry with God." ▪

Leonardo DiCaprio said that he has made a donation to UNICEF for tsunami relief in Thailand, where he spent four months shooting the 2000 movie "The Beach."

Charities seeing 'unprecedented' levels of giving for tsunami victims

By Richard Huff and Dave Goldiner

New York Daily News
NEW YORK

Spurred by horrific images of devastation, Americans—famous and ordinary—are donating so much cash that charities are being swamped by their generosity. One maxed-out agency actually is telling donors they have enough money, and charity officials say the outpouring has reminded them of the surge in donations following the Sept. 11 tragedy.

"This is unprecedented," said Oxfam America spokesman Nathaniel Raymond, struggling to find a way to compare it to past crises. "It's like comparing the Amazon to the Charles River here in Boston," he concluded.

Actress Sandra Bullock, who starred in Miss Congeniality, started the most recent gusher by promising to give $1 million to the relief effort.

The figure matched the amount she gave to victims after the Sept. 11 terror attacks.

Leonardo DiCaprio also kicked in an unspecified "large" donation.

DiCaprio shot his 2000 thriller The Beach on the Thai resort island of Phi Phi, which was ravaged by quake-spawned waves.

And NBC boss Jeff Zucker announced that the network will air a prime-time relief telethon starring "Sex and the City" star Sarah Jessica Parker, "American Idol" singer Clay Aiken and "Will and Grace" actress Debra Messing.

Even as the rich and famous stepped up to the plate, charities say they can hardly keep up with the millions of dollars in online donations from ordinary Americans.

French firefighters observe three minutes of silence outside the Saint Sulpice church as people throughout Europe hold a silent tribute to the victims of the Indian Ocean tsunami.

The American Red Cross already has logged $79 million in donations. Oxfam has logged $12 million—and counting.

Doctors Without Borders was so swamped with gifts that it started referring donors to other charities.

People surround a bus as they stand for a silent tribute in front of the EU Council building in Brussels, Wednesday Jan. 5, 2005. Stock exchanges, workers, and businesses held a silent tribute across much of Europe to remember the victims of the Indian Ocean tsunami.

The American Jewish World Service received $2 million online. In all of last year, the group got $40,000 through its Web site.

"We're just so grateful for the help that's allowing us to do our work and help the people who are suffering," said Jackie Flowers of the Red Cross.

Touched by the far-reaching misery, kids have emptied their piggy banks and poverty-stricken seniors handed over the $5 they could spare.

Charities call the tsunami disaster the first catastrophe of the Internet age. Unlike past disasters like the 1984 Ethiopian famine that grew over months, the tidal waves exploded instantly on the world's television screens.

Instead of having to write a check, lick a stamp and send off a donation, Americans are logging on and click-

Plai Sudlor, a 25-year-old male elephant, walks through a bush with its keeper Nimit Insamran during a searching mission for bodies of tsunami victims at a rambutan plantation in Bang Niang village in Takuapa district of Pang-Nga province, southern Thailand, Monday, Jan. 3, 2005. Forensic experts have begun exhuming 300 tsunami victims in Thailand after discovering their bodies apparently were mislabeled.

ing their gifts in a matter of seconds.

"The Internet is fast, it's impulsive," said Ronni Strongin of the American Jewish World Service, which funnels the aid to 24 partner groups in south Asia. "People want to react and they want to react now." ▪

Nicobari girls play at a tsunami relief camp in Port Blair in India's southeastern Andaman and Nicobar Islands archipelago, Wednesday, Jan. 5, 2005. The tsunami has severely damaged parts of the archipelago, with some islands breaking up, land masses tilting and underwater coral reefs emerging above the sea. Indira Point, the farthest tip of the Indian territory, may have just completely disappeared, say army surveyors and survivors.

Relief workers
focus on battered souls By Hugh Dellios

Chicago Tribune

BANDA ACEH, Indonesia

In the refugee camp, the young woman named Yunidar sits in silence, occasionally talking to herself. She has been that way since she lived through the cruelest moment of the tsunami disaster in Southeast Asia.

When the water came, Yunidar, 30, grabbed two of her three young sons under her arms and ran. But she was engulfed by a torrent over her head.

"I lost my grip," she says, telling the tale in a monotone voice that suddenly accelerates into a panicked plea and gulps of air.

Ultimately, the two sons drowned and a third son and her husband are missing. But it was the wrenching of the two from her motherly embrace—a horrifying ordeal told by parents across the region—that haunts Yunidar the most.

With basic relief efforts now under way, rescue workers are beginning to focus on trying to help tsunami victims like Yunidar cope with what they saw and endured, as well as the waves of grief, mourning and guilt that have washed over them in the past two weeks.

Many of the international assistance groups in Indonesia, Sri Lanka and elsewhere say that teams of psychologists and sociologists will begin arriving to deal with the mental and emotional toll of the killer wave that killed more than 155,000.

They will find no end of potential patients, including the fisherman standing on his intact boat, "Sailing the Sea," in the Banda Aceh harbor. He blankly stared off at mile after square mile of devastation, able to respond only with head nods to questions about the family he will never see again.

Aid groups have mounting lists of cases. An official with Save the Children told of a 16-year-old youth who the sea spit back onto the beach with a broken leg. Unable to move, he lay there for three days with another survivor, who eventually died and was eaten by dogs.

"This is the time when people really recoil into themselves," said Ron Waldman, a World Health Organization official in Banda Aceh. "Right now, we're trying to first prevent outbreaks of diseases, but not because it's more important than the psycho-social aspects. It's just that the solutions are easier."

Waldman and others emphasize the long-term nature of addressing psychological trauma. He said different victims deal with it in generally three ways. Some are "utterly incapacitated with depression and post-traumatic syndrome, people so blown away they will need medical attention," he said.

A second group will need counseling to help them grieve.

A third group, Waldman said, will adjust simply with the redevelopment of their old, familiar community, after the rebuilding of mosques and schools, getting back to their jobs or restoring the fishing fleets.

The northern part of Sumatra island, where Banda Aceh is, is a deeply Muslim region. For that reason, most victims—including Yunidar—see the tragedy in terms of God's will and are more likely to respond to a sermon at the mosque than to Western-style counseling.

"I think if you want to share this story, it's not with other people. It's with God," she said, as several wide-eyed children sat around her on the ground in front of her tent. "I pray to God, and then I feel calm. There must be a rea-

An Indian police officer tries to control hungry survivors of the tsunami as rice is handed out at a relief camp in Devanah Pattinam, India. The truck had to leave midway as chaos prevailed as there was not enough rice to be distributed to all the evacuees of the camp.

son for what happened."

Other victims sought that solitude during services at the city's main mosque, the five-domed Mesjid Raya Baiturrahman. Religious officials and soldiers had raced to repair and open it for the first time since the disaster.

"We are sad and in grief, but Islam taught us to be optimistic in seeing the future," imam Din Syamsuddin said in his sermon. "People in crisis will say, 'I am owned by God, I come from God and I will be returned to God.' This is the therapy of Islam."

That way of thinking, repeated over and over here, helped many explain the disaster. It helped others alleviate the guilty feelings that have wedged themselves into mourners' grief.

Yulianto, 48, an Education Ministry worker, said he had seen "signs" that a disaster was coming in the days before

Geophysicists with the National Weather Service Pacific Tsunami Warning Center, Barry Hirshorn, foreground, and Stuart Weinstein, monitor computer tracking systems watching for tsunami, or tidal wave activity in the Pacific Ocean, in Ewa Beach, Hawaii. India will search for the best technology available to set up an early warning system to protect the country from future tsunamis.

the earthquake that created the tsunami. Still, he did not flee with his family, and his wife and daughter were killed.

"I know about tsunamis. My car is in front of the house, prepared to go and everything, but we didn't leave," he said, visiting the shorefront where his house once stood for the first time Thursday. "That's why we believe this is God's plan."

At the refugee camp, Yunidar's neighbors whisper

An overturned cargo ship is seen in this aerial view of the town of Meulaboh in Aceh province, Indonesia, which was flattened by tidal waves.

about her, that she spends so much time by herself, that she rarely speaks. They say she sits and thinks about what happened to her, over and over again.

Such a tale was horrifyingly common in the wake of the tsunami. One mother told a global satellite television channel that she will never forget the look in her children's eyes as they broke from her grasp and disappeared under the water.

Waldman, the WHO official, said the loss of a child or children from a parents' own hands "is always the most dramatic tragedy. Floods do this, although not on this scale." It sometimes happens in war too, he said.

Yunidar said she regrets that she prevented her 7-year-old, Aidil Chalis, from running off to find his father as he wanted when the water came. He and her 7-month-old baby, Farhan Irhani, were the two who slipped from her

A Red Cross worker, right, holds a bucket accepting donations to the disaster relief fund for the tsunami victims as fans enter the stadium for the Baltimore Ravens – Miami Dolphins football game in Baltimore Sunday, Jan. 2, 2005. The Baltimore Ravens pledged $15,000 and promised to match an additional $10,000 collected from fans at the team's game against the visiting Miami Dolphins on Sunday.

grasp.

Her husband, Bahrun, and 3-year-old, Fakrun Nizam, are missing.

Yunidar says she finds some solace in knowing that she eventually found the bodies of the first two children and was able to bathe them before burying them.

"My task as a mother and a Muslim is fulfilled," she said. ■

A boy prepares to somersault as he plays into a pile of clothes donated by people for the tsunami affected people, left out to dry in the compound of a temple, in Nagappattinam, in the south Indian state of Tamil Nadu, India, Sunday, Jan. 9, 2005.

Sri Lankans who lost all discover shelter at school By Kim Barker

Chicago Tribune

PANADURA, Sri Lanka

The two teenage girls sleep with 38 other people on the floor of classroom 6-B, near school desks holding all they recovered from the wreckage of their lives: some clothes, some towels and two waterlogged folders holding medical records. "For a baby," one reads. Infant pictures are pasted on the other.

Sadeeka Kalpani, 18, is eight months pregnant. Jayangani Peiris, 15, is to deliver twins in about two months. They are always together in this refugee camp, often appearing swollen and uncomfortable.

Sometimes, they totter to meals or tea, their bellies far in front of them. But mostly they sit in the shade of their classroom and worry about what might happen.

"There's no shortage of food," Kalpani said. "But we worry about the future of our babies. They don't have anything here. We don't have baby clothes, or baby food, or a mosquito net for a baby."

About 2,200 people live in this refugee camp at St. John's College, the largest makeshift shelter in Kalutara district, just south of the capital Colombo. Many who live here, as in the rest of the Sri Lanka, lost everything when the tsunami crashed into the coast Dec. 26.

A day in the life of this shelter shows just how difficult it is to care for so many people with so many needs, from the pregnant teens such as Peiris and Kalpani to the children with scrapes to the elderly who stare into space. Some children go to the bathroom in the courtyard and run around naked or nearly so. Everyone asks visitors for money. One girl painstakingly writes out her address in English for journalists, as if she wants them to visit. But her house is no longer there.

This place provides food, shelter and water. But other needs, such as counseling or financial help, will have to wait.

St. John's, usually a Christian school for children, now looks like a small city. Clothes dry on banisters and desks. Boys play cricket in the yard. Refugees wait in line for haircuts, meals and tea. When new donations arrive, people stand in line for them.

Doctors stop by for checkups. The army stops to make sure there are no problems. Politicians stop to ask questions.

Life here can be measured in announcements, made over the school's public address system every five minutes by D.B. Gerald Fernando, 63, a retired government worker. In a monotone, he tells people what to do. For the barber, go to one end of campus, starting at 12:15 p.m. For clean water, go to the other end.

Pregnant women should line up for water thermoses at 1:30 p.m. and sheets at 4:30 p.m. Lights should be out by 9:30 p.m.

People such as Renuka Gamampila stop by the camp, full of hope and fear. They ask Fernando to announce the names of missing relatives. Gamampila is searching for her sister and waits for 10 minutes after the announcement. No one comes.

"We've been told she's alive, but no one can find her," Gamampila said.

All day long, Fernando calls out the most important

A Thai elephant clears debris near Bang Nieng beach in Khao Lak, Thailand. Elephants were used to join the huge effort to clean up Thailand's southern coastline to clear debris.

piece of advice he knows: "Wash your hands, wash your hands, wash your hands." So far, there have been no cases of diarrhea here, no scabies, no chickenpox. The medical staff tries to be vigilant.

"We've been lucky," said Dr. Anil Dissanayake, regional director of health services in the Kalutara district.

About a week after the disaster, the St. John's camp was somewhat organized, unlike many others in the country, set up in temples, mosques, churches and schools. St. John's is less than an hour's drive from Colombo, so trucks can easily drop off food and clothing. The school principal, A.D. Karunarathna, treats the refugees like new students, registering each person and making a file.

"I decided we had to do everything we could for people," Karunarathna said. "We had to treat them with respect. Most of all, we had to listen to them."

The problems are overwhelming. Although tens of thousands of people died in the tsunami in Sri Lanka, only a few perished along the 18 miles of coast here between Moratuwa and Kalutara. But 4,000 homes, mostly concrete boxes and wooden squatter huts, were flattened. And 14,000 people, many the families of poor fishermen and woodcarvers, lost everything.

When the water came, Kalpani was in her kitchen, cooking string hoppers, a Sri Lankan dish, to sell on the beach. She shared the two-room house on the beach with nine relatives.

Peiris had been working in the family shop a mile away, pickling relish to sell. About 9:30 a.m. on that Sunday, someone ran down the beach, shouting that the water was rough, and that people should leave their homes. Kalpani walked as fast as she could, holding her belly, to a temple on higher ground. She wore a dress, no shoes and a Buddhist copper charm believed to protect against evil.

"Most people were running past me," Kalpani said. "I'm pregnant. So with the greatest difficulty, I walked away really, really fast."

After Peiris heard about the water, she started shouting for help. Two women helped carry her to higher ground. She watched as the water swallowed homes and spit out pieces of roofing and furniture.

"I was thinking about what might happen," Peiris said. "I thought I was going to die, and I thought my babies were going to die." Both teens' husbands survived the waves.

About this time, Karunarathna, on Christmas vacation and miles away from the coast, heard about the disaster. Aware that his large school was on high ground, he called the school's custodian. "Open the gates," he said. "Open all the doors. Let everyone in."

When Karunarathna arrived at the school the day of the tsunami, he was shocked by what he saw. Thousands of people huddled together. There was no first aid, no sleeping mats, no coordination. People were frightened. The sun was starting to set. Karunarathna bought bulbs and wiring, and strung up makeshift lights.

He met with health officials and printed up a form for families to fill out. Each person was given a number–Kalpani was No. 40, Peiris 203. Karunarathna worried about other problems: The school had only nine toilets for 32 classrooms. Within a day, outhouses were set up. Water and food started arriving. And by the end of the week, people seemed to suffer more from the weight of not knowing what would happen than from lack of food.

Peiris and Kalpani sat in their dingy classroom, on the third floor of the school, in the shadow of students' old drawings of food groups.

"The future is so uncertain," Kalpani said. "I hope things get better, but until everything calms down, we have to stay here. We don't want to. We have no choice." ■

Passing a huge tug boat washed up on the main coastal road of the island by the massive tsunamis, a young girl carries supplies back on the three day walk to her village inaccessible by washed out roads.

Athletes step up
to help tsunami victims By Jena Janovy

Knight Ridder Newspapers

CHARLOTTE, N.C.

Some of the world's top athletes are showing us what it means to be role models and sports heroes. Since the tsunami struck Asia on Dec. 26, a disaster that has killed hundreds of thousands, some of the world's top athletes and a number of sports organizations have stepped forward with significant donations for relief efforts.

There are countless athletes who have contributed. Count among them American tennis players Andy Roddick and Venus Williams and Russian Wimbledon champion Maria Sharapova. The NFL, NBA, and Major League Baseball have all seen contributions from both individual players and owners, as well as the leagues themselves.

The glory of sports is that athletes and teams are perfectly positioned to call upon fans to help, too. Sports events draw thousands who can be asked for spare change as they enter a sporting venue. They've responded, too.

The Charlotte Bobcats and New Jersey Nets are among NBA teams that have collected donations from fans. Wingate collected money at recent college basketball games to send to the American Red Cross International Response Fund.

Outside stadiums, American Red Cross volunteers with buckets collected donations from fans attending the Rose Bowl and Cotton Bowl.

There are other examples of similar efforts going on all around this country, and it's one of the most rewarding, inspiring, meaningful sights you'll see—and be able to show your kids.

We like to talk of our sports figures as heroes. We view them as invincible and capable of great feats. We play backyard football, driveway basketball and video games, pretending we're them. We ogle at the sums of money they take home, the multimillion-dollar contracts that let them buy big houses, custom-built cars and blinding jewelry.

We've seen them fall though, too, with heartbreaking losses, violent outbursts on the court or run-ins with the law off the field, and it sometimes makes us wonder what kind of people they really are—who are these athletes we're holding up as great role models for our children?

Now is a perfect opportunity to talk to your kids about heroes, to teach them the value of human life and the importance of understanding what is going on in the world around them. Talk to them about how they are fortunate to live at a time and in a country where they can be in a position to help others, whether it's to help with tsunami relief or other problems closer to home. There are plenty of needs in the United States, and athletes often are at the forefront of relief for those causes, as well.

Of all the wins and losses our sports heroes have bestowed upon us over the generations, these are the kinds of efforts that will be remembered as the greatest victories we've ever witnessed. ■

Workers load relief supplies sent by the local Karnataka government onto an Indian Air Force aircraft to be sent to Andaman and Nicobar Islands tsunami victims.

Drug companies donating supplies in unprecedented amounts By Linda Loyd

Knight Ridder Newspapers

PHILADELPHIA

The outpouring of cash and supplies by corporations—and pharmaceutical and health-care products companies in particular—is surpassing donations to victims in any previous natural disaster, or even the Sept. 11, 2001, attacks, relief agencies say. In all, health-care companies have announced donations totaling at least $72 million so far.

A FedEx airplane recently left Washington Dulles International Airport packed with $1.5 million worth of donated medicines and medical supplies. The shipment, destined for Jakarta, Indonesia, and sponsored by Project Hope, contained everything from antibiotics, antiviral drugs and skin-infection ointments donated by GlaxoSmithKline to bandages and surgical dressings from Johnson & Johnson.

By the end of that week (Jan. 9), FedEx expected to have shipped 200 tons of medical supplies, first aid products and portable medical laboratories to Sri Lanka and Indonesia, spokesman Pam Roberson said. United Parcel Service said it is prepared to ship up to 1 million pounds of emergency relief supplies weekly via air, ocean and ground from Europe, Asia and the Americas. UPS put the value of those services at $2.5 million.

With gifts of items from scalpels, syringes and bandages to anti-diarrhea medicines, nutritional supplements, cough medicine, and rehydration treatments, humanitarian groups say the flow of medicines and cash is the greatest ever seen, said Ken Baker, director of corporate relations for AmeriCares. His group has sent a plane of medicines to Sri Lanka and soon will airlift medicines

and supplies into India and Indonesia.

"Pharmaceutical companies are asking what we need. They are not telling us what they have available. It's extraordinary," said Martin Smith, spokesman for Map International of Brunswick, Ga., a nonprofit organization that plans to airlift 10 cargo containers of medicines and supplies to help tsunami victims.

Baker, of AmeriCares in Stamford, Conn., said GlaxoSmithKline has an ongoing program to supply several nonprofit relief agencies with a $7 million line of credit to choose products—such as antibiotics, anti-parasitics and anti-ulcer drugs—to keep in charities' warehouses, available to ship immediately in any disaster. "It's unprecedented for us to see that kind of line of corporate credit," he said.

Glaxo has donated 2 million doses of antibiotics for tsunami relief, and 600,000 vials of hepatitis A and typhoid vaccines, as well as $3.8 million in cash for relief efforts. The drug maker said its antibiotics have already been airlifted to Sri Lanka, India and Indonesia by AmeriCares.

Merck & Co. Inc. has given $3 million in cash to relief agencies and will donate medicines as needed, said spokeswoman Anita Larsen.

Among the biggest corporate givers is Pfizer Inc., which is providing $10 million in cash and $25 million in medicines. "Local authorities are telling us they need painkillers, antibiotics and antifungals" for skin infections, said Paula Luff, Pfizer senior director of international philanthropy, in an interview.

The world's largest pharmaceutical company, Pfizer has offices in all Asian countries affected by the tsunami disaster, except Sri Lanka, and is donating medicines

Willie Nelson performs during the "Tsunami Relief Austin to South Asia" concert at the Austin Music Hall in Austin, Texas, Sunday, Jan. 9, 2005. Proceeds from the $25 tickets will go to the Red Cross, UNICEF and Doctors Without Borders organizations.

Many sources, like wells, have been contaminated by seawater, debris and sewage. Procter & Gamble has given 9.8 million packets of powder to purify drinking water and sold another 6 million packets to relief groups at steeply discounted prices.

Wyeth has donated $1 million, and given antibiotics, vaccines, anti-inflammatory products, nutritionals and analgesics. Wyeth is also donating over-the-counter consumer products, such as Advil, Dimetapp and Robitussin.

Israel-based Teva Pharmaceutical Industries Ltd., a generic drug maker with its U.S. headquarters in North Wales, has shipped 40 tons of medicines, including antibiotics, first aid creams, and painkillers to Thailand via relief organizations in Israel.

Relief agencies do not expect problems from outdated donated pharmaceuticals or oversupplies of medicines that plagued past humanitarian disasters in Kosovo and Bosnia. The World Health Organization issued guidelines in 1996 to deter companies from donating any drug that is within one year of its expiration date and to limit donations only to drugs specifically requested by recipients.

"We don't accept outdated products," said Martin Smith of Map International. "We ask for long-dated supplies, products that won't expire for many months."

Baker acknowledged the problems of outdated, inappropriate or otherwise unusable drugs and medical supplies in the '80s and '90s have led those involved in humanitarian aid to be more vigilant.

Baker said a coalition of agencies and pharmaceutical companies was formed in the late 1990s "to insure all donations sent out are appropriate, needed, and will be used." ▪

from supplies already in Thailand, India, Malaysia and Indonesia. Pfizer employees in those countries are delivering medicines to hospitals and local governments directly. "The medicine labels are in their language," she said. "If we exhaust local supplies, we have a supply point in Hong Kong."

Project Hope president and CEO John Howe said doctors are seeing crush injuries, lung infection and now pneumonia and dysentery–especially in Banda Aceh, Indonesia, which was hard-hit by the tsunami.

"The immediate needs, particularly in Indonesia, are for antibiotics, syringes, intravenous lines, catheters, bandages, dressings and surgical tape to respond to the injuries and infections," Howe said.

Fresh drinking water is one of the items most needed.

Nataya Pumsi, 36, looks at the boat that landed on her house and destroyed it after the village of Ban Nam Khem was hit by the tsunami in Khao Lak in southern Thailand.

Indonesia's tsunami death toll nears 210,000 by Tim Johnson

Knight Ridder Newspapers
BANDA ACEH, Indonesia

An official document posted here says that nearly 210,000 people in Indonesia are dead or missing from the Dec. 26 tsunami, a death toll that appears to be far higher than officials have reported publicly. Rescue workers think even that number may be low.

The larger Indonesia toll would bring the total of dead and missing from the tidal surge across the Indian Ocean to nearly 272,000, ranking the tsunami as the fifth or sixth deadliest natural disaster in about 250 years.

The new death toll came as Indonesian officials restricted the movements of foreign relief workers, U.N. employees and journalists in devastated north Sumatra, the Indonesian island that took the brunt of the tsunami's force, and said foreign military units would be allowed to work in the country for only a limited time.

Indonesia's vice president told the United States and other nations that have sent troops to deliver relief that their forces won't be permitted to remain in Sumatra longer than three months, and should leave as soon as their work is completed.

The chief of operations for the government's disaster-relief efforts here, Budi Atmadi Adiputro, said in a statement that it was "necessary" for all foreigners in Aceh province, at the northern end of Sumatra, to provide authorities with details of "their current and planned activities as well as the exact locations those activities will be carried out."

The blunt comments seemed to end what had been tacit Indonesian acceptance of a foreign presence in an area that has been off limits to foreigners for years. But it wasn't clear that the comments would have any real impact on rescue efforts.

Few civilian relief workers seemed concerned that the restrictions would hurt their missions, and Indonesian officials promised quick approval for missions outside of Aceh's principal cities.

U.S. aircraft continued to fly relief missions, though helicopters from the aircraft carrier Abraham Lincoln had to refuel elsewhere after the Lincoln moved out of Indonesian waters after the Indonesian government refused permission for U.S. training flights over its territory.

Indonesia, which emerged from three decades of military dictatorship in 1998, remains strongly influenced by the armed forces, some of whose officers are discomfited by the sudden presence of foreigners in a conflict-ridden province that's the source of huge earnings from natural gas exports.

Human rights groups have long complained of the military's crackdown on separatists from the Free Aceh Movement, and the United States ended military exchanges over the issue during the Clinton administration. Tensions over the presence of foreign troops have been obvious for days, with U.S. Marines scaling back planned operations after the Indonesians objected to the Marines' carrying weapons on Indonesian territory.

Indonesian officials offered no explanation for the sharp rise in the number of dead and missing. Earlier this week, a Cabinet-level official put the toll in Aceh province at about 108,000, between those already

Devastation to Banda Aceh city in the Indonesian province of Aceh is observed from a U.S. Navy helicopter.

buried and those known to be dead. Another 48,000 were missing, the official said.

But a chart posted at the entrance to the federal disaster-relief headquarters here offered different numbers.

Compiled by the Disaster Management Task Force for Aceh province, the document listed numbers of casualties by district in a variety of categories, including buried, known dead and missing.

The document gave the number of people known to have died in the disaster at 78,395 and said another 131,479 remained lost or missing. It said the information was current as of 9 a.m. EST Jan. 12.

Asked about the document, an American working for the Indonesian government, Laura Worsley-Brown,

Debris are scattered around a standing mosque at Banda Aceh, the capital of Aceh province, Tuesday, Jan. 11, 2005, more than two weeks after a devastating tsunami ravaged the capital and other coastal towns in northwest Indonesia. Houses and other buildings are no match to the force of the devastating tsunami but mosques are practically intact.

said it was posted in response to reporters' inquiries about the numbers of dead and missing and was being offered in place of official statements.

Those returning from the field said they weren't surprised by the new numbers. Dr. A. John Watson, the president of CARE Canada, cited the town of Calang, halfway between the provincial capital of

A wide area of destruction is shown from an aerial shot Sunday Jan. 2, 2005 of Meulaboh, 56 Miles west of Banda Aceh, the capital of Aceh province in northwest Indonesia following the earthquake-triggered Tsunami.

Banda Aceh and Meulaboh, which is on the western coast, as "a really hard-hit case. Eight or nine thousand people in that town were wiped out. About 1,000 survived." He said he expected the final death toll to be "significantly higher."

The precise death toll is unlikely ever to be known. Thousands of people were washed to sea, and their bodies probably never will be recovered.

But the new figures rank the tsunami in the same category as a 1976 earthquake in China that killed at least 255,000 people. The worst natural disaster since 1750 is thought to have been a flood in China in 1939 that killed an estimated 3.7 million people.

(above) Volunteers place dry ice on corpses in a mass grave Friday, Jan. 7, 2005, at Wat Bang Muang, near Takuapa, Thailand. Hundreds of thousands of people are listed dead. (right) An aerial view of a bridge damaged by the Dec. 26 tsunami in the eastern town of Pottuvil, Sri Lanka.

The travel restrictions announced Wednesday apply to all foreigners, including "individuals, country representatives, United Nations agencies, NGOs (nongovernmental organizations), or media in Aceh province," the government statement said.

The government said it acted out of concern that insurgents of the Free Aceh Movement might under-

take violent acts and said military escorts would be provided in certain cases.

But aid workers said authorities might fear that relief groups or journalists would help the insurgents, who've been fighting for independence for the province since 1976.

Alwi Shihab, a Cabinet-level appointee of President Susilo Bambang Yudhoyono, declined to say what would occur to individuals or groups that didn't register.

"We are sure you are civilized persons and will comply with regulations for your own safety," Shihab said.

The announcement said foreigners were free to work in and around the two hardest-hit cities, Banda Aceh and Meulaboh, a city near the epicenter of the massive quake and tsunami. For other locations, foreigners must send a request to a team led by the Aceh regional police chief and await a decision.

"It will not take long," Shihab said. "It will be within hours, not days."

Aceh has been largely off-limits to foreigners since

An aerial view of an uninhabited island whose beach has been washed by tidal waves, as seen from an Indian Air force AN32 plane at Nicobar, in India's southeastern Andaman and Nicobar Islands. It has also wiped out scores of villages, altered entire islands, and created mountains of debris that could choke mangrove forests and destroy coral reefs.

early 2003, when a cease-fire broke down and martial law was declared. Shihab noted that a lower-level emergency rule that permits restricted civil liberties remains in effect.

Reaction among foreign relief officials ranged from concern about security in the countryside to apprehension that the government may be allowing security concerns to trump humanitarian needs.

Most, however, appeared so intent on providing aid to as many as 650,000 displaced people in Aceh that they took the restrictions as simply another hurdle in an already difficult situation. ■

This picture released by the U.S. Navy shows an aerial view of the tsunami-stricken coastal region near Aceh, Sumatra, Indonesia in the Indian Ocean.

Children of Sri Lanka in shock, wonderment at their own survival
By Lennox Samuels

The Dallas Morning News
KALMUNAI, Sri Lanka

She'd been stoic, almost cheerful, at her uncle's house earlier in the day, but as the 10-year-old girl approached the stretch of brown sand, she stopped cold. "I don't want to see the sea anymore," she pleaded, clutching her elder cousin's arm with both hands.

The poise disappeared and her face crumpled in grief as she stared, terrified, at the beach where she had played every day for most of her life and at the now-placid water that days before had taken away her mother.

"I want to move away from here," whispered Thanucia Navendran.

Of the more than 150,000 people who lost their lives in the tsunamis that struck this region, about a third were children. But beyond that statistic are thousands more children who lost cousins, aunts, grandmothers or a parent—or two—in the disaster.

As authorities keep talking about how many billions of dollars have been pledged to countries devastated by the killer wave, more and more adults worry about the children in places like Sri Lanka, where more than 30,000 perished.

Many of those children continue to grapple with their experiences as they pass the time with surviving relatives or in refugee camps. These are some of their stories.

Kopika Arulrasa, a shy 9-year-old, is at first reluctant to speak, as she stands in the yard at Ramakrishna Mission School, which now serves as a refugee center for 1,100 tsunami survivors. About 160 are children.

The long-haired girl, wearing a light-colored dress—or "frock" as they still say in this former British colony—was at Hindu services earlier and has a dash of powder on her forehead, much like Christians on Ash Wednesday.

"I was playing near my auntie's house, and I saw the water level in the sea had climbed to around 10 meters (32.8 feet)," she says. "And it was moving toward land.

"At first, I thought somewhere it must be raining. But my elder sister shouted, 'Sea coming! Sea coming!'

"I started to run when the water level is around waist-high.

"Then the second wave strikes. I was thrown out, but I managed to hold on to a branch of a kukumba tree, and I escaped."

Nearby, Jasinthan Rasamani, 8, looks quizzically at the 10 of diamonds in his hand as he plays cards with fellow youngsters seated at a weather-beaten wooden table. Two brown bandages describe an X on the right side of the boy's forehead. He was injured while running to safety.

On Dec. 26, his mother and his younger brother, Tino, had gone to church, leaving Jasinthan playing with some friends in front of the family home.

The boy realized, he says, that the water looked different from the way it normally does. Not just at a higher level, but darker, more churning.

This photo provided by the United Nations shows an aerial view of the destruction left in the wake of the Asian tsunami between Hambantota and Trincomalee, Sri Lanka.

An aerial shot taken from a US Navy Seahawk helicopter from carrier USS Abraham Lincoln, shows a barge and a tugboat swept ashore by the Dec. 26 Tsunami near the coastal town of Lamno, south of Banda Aceh.

"Scary."

He turned toward town and started to run, just a few yards ahead of the encroaching Indian Ocean.

He tripped and fell.

"I thought the water would catch me then," he said, frowning at the cards in his hand. "But anyway, I got away."

Kirubai Prasad, 12, had gone the day before to see Sri Murugan Kovil, a respected Hindu seer. He had stayed out late at the festival, until about 2 a.m., and so he slept in.

"I woke up when I felt water pouring on the bed," he says.

"I thought somebody in my family was pouring water to wake me up.

"I turned on to the other side of the bed and went back to sleep again and a little after that the water came again.

"The water pushed me onto the roof.

"It was unbelievable.

"I cannot forget it."

The tidal wave took Ajantha Yogeswaran's mother, her 10-year-old twin sisters, Janani and Jalani, and her grandmother.

"On the day, just after I took a bath, I was ready to change my clothes when my amma—"mother" in Tamil—shouted from our shop, which is attached in front of our main hall, that the sea was coming to the house," says the 17-year-old.

"Then everything happened. In a whisker of time, I saw the bathroom break down into pieces of bricks," she says, crying quietly.

"I was thrown onto the roof by the wave and then the next wave threw me into a coconut tree. My hair got stuck into the leaves, which I think saved me from death."

She doesn't know how the rest of her family per-

Aerial shot from United States Navy helicopter shows damage, caused by the quake and tsunami, to Kuede Teunom on the north eastern coast of the Indonesian.

People walk past a boat swept ashore by the force of tsunami at Nagapattinam, India.

ished exactly, but doesn't care to speculate either.

"I feel very bad now," she says, standing on what once was the floor of her bedroom. "But I've got to complete my studies and continue the rest of the life, and I need to look after my younger brother, too.

"After this tsunami, I realize life is nothing; any time it can be demolished.

"This sea might come again," she says, waving at the surf. "We want to avoid it. I even hate to look at it."

Thanucia Navendran and her classmates were rehearsing a dance for a program at their Sunday religious school.

"Suddenly, I saw boats ... crashing with each other and heard a horrible noise coming suddenly and the sea moving toward our school," she said.

The teacher at Kalmunai Sri Mamangam Vidyalayam School went to the stage and shouted instructions at her students, telling them to climb onto the stage to get away from the water, which was rising rapidly.

"I ran to safety to escape from it, and I was holding the hand of Nishanthan, my neighbor, who is 5 years old. I was able to move inside a house on the way.

"The first wave threw me, and I grabbed the shoulder of Seedevi Akka, who was grabbing the steel window in search of safety.

"On the way, I lost the young one. (The boy died after swallowing muddy and salty seawater.) After the second wave attack, which was worse, I was thrown around, but my uncle found me and took me to Kalmunai hospital.

"My mother and 11 out of 13 Sunday school teachers died, along with a dozen of the students. I don't know how I lived. It is all like mystery and shock.

"Most of the people ran for safety by calling the name of Mamanga Pillyar—save us," she says, referring to the Hindu temple near her school.

That entreaty was never granted. Near the very spot where Thanucia stands describing her experiences, the temple itself lies in shambles.

The Kalmunai beach is choked with debris, the only visitors the odd fisherman checking to see whether the fish are biting, and a group of crows that caw incessantly. A red bucket sits on a mound where another tsunami casualty—a child—is buried. Part of a skull and bits of vertebrae are still visible on a blackened bit of earth where a body was cremated.

At Base Hospital, a baby boy, 3 to 5 months old, wails as a nurse tries to comfort him. A man deposited him at the hospital the afternoon of Dec. 26, after the water finally had receded.

Five couples have come forward to claim the boy. Officials expect the matter to be settled in court.

In the meantime, they call the child Tsunami. ∎

An aerial image taken from a helicopter shows villagers standing next to a road destroyed by the tsunami at Telwatte, about 63 miles south of Colombo, Sri Lanka.

As tsunami death toll climbs past 150,000, relief efforts starting to jell

By Ken Moritsugu and Ben Stocking

Knight Ridder Newspapers
JAKARTA, Indonesia

Two weeks after the tsunami hit, the official death toll continues to rise, topping 150,000 as bodies were uncovered during the massive clean-up on the Indonesian island of Sumatra.

At the same time, however, the massive international aid effort seems to have found its legs. Major relief efforts often become "chaotic," said Pat Johns, the emergency response coordinator for Catholic Relief Services, but "this time, it's going well."

And the World Health Organization said that no major disease outbreaks have been reported in the crowded refugee camps housing survivors.

Indonesia added another 2,737 people to the list of the confirmed dead, raising the number of victims in that country to 104,055 and pushing the global total over 150,000.

The hardest hit area stretches from Banda Aceh, a city at the northern tip of Sumatra, to the town of Meulaboh, about 125 miles down the coast, according to an initial assessment by a United Nations team. Further south, the U.N. team found that "the damage is less severe, but people are still in need of assistance."

The Indonesian government raised its estimate of the homeless to 655,132, but the actual number won't be known until a full survey of the coast can be carried out.

The United Nations' World Food Program is feeding about 130,000 refugees in Sumatra, with plans to start distributing a one-month supply of rice, beans and other food to another 140,000 over the weekend. If the government's estimate of the homeless is accurate, it means the food is reaching less than half of the people displaced by the tsunami.

World governments led by Australia, Japan, Germany and the United States have pledged almost $4 billion in aid, and private donations to relief groups add to the total resources becoming available.

At Banda Aceh, sacks of rice and boxes of biscuits are stacked high. Trucks rumble in and out of the World Food Program warehouse with signs on the front: CARE, World Vision, Mercy Corps.

United Nations agencies are in place, the major private relief organizations are hard at work and the U.S. military is playing a major logistical role, shuttling supplies up and down the coast in helicopters.

Military detachments from across the globe—Portugal, Spain, Pakistan, Germany—are also here supporting the effort, as are an array of Indonesian aid organizations.

With communications knocked out and transportation systems leveled, it took several days for the relief effort to get up to speed.

"Emergencies are always complex," said Eileen Burke of Save the Children.

"You always come across hiccups that slow your progress. You resolve them and move on."

The United Nations is doing the coordinating, holding daily meetings with dozens of relief groups from around the globe.

The humanitarian assistance is easy to see now, with trucks unloading food and supplies all around Banda Aceh, the hub of the relief effort. Cargo planes come and go and helicopters thunder overhead all day, delivering supplies along the coast, where dozens of towns were wiped out.

A man searches the debris that litters the tsunami damaged city of Meulaboh on the island of Sumatra, Indonesia.

Also, U.N. Secretary General Kofi Annan traveled to Sri Lanka to see the devastation there. Sri Lanka, with 30,000 killed, is the second-hardest hit country after Indonesia.

"We came to listen and to learn and I think you have given ... (us) some ideas," Annan told local officials.

More than 800,000 Sri Lankans were left homeless by the tsunami, and most will need food aid. The World Food Program has brought in enough food—rice, lentils and sugar—to feed 750,000 people for 15 days, the U.N. agency said.

"There is now enough food around Sri Lanka to feed everyone who needs it," said Jeff Taft-Dick, the World Food Program director in Sri Lanka. But he added that the relief effort is "only just beginning," as his agency believes that most of the homeless will need food aid for six months.

President Bush devoted his weekly radio address to reviewing U.S. efforts to help tsunami victims. He termed the $350 million in pledged federal aid "an initial commitment" and again encouraged Americans to

(above) An aerial shot taken from a helicopter shows boats stranded on the shore after the powerful tidal wave in the coastal town Galle, Sri Lanka. (right) An aerial view of the harbor that was destroyed and fishing boats piled against the bridge by tsunamis at a fishermen's colony, in Nagappattinam, in the southern Indian state of Tamil Nadu.

donate cash to private relief groups such as the Red Cross, CARE and Catholic Relief Services. He noted that he recently signed legislation permitting Americans to deduct cash contributions for tsunami relief from their 2004 federal income tax.

Humanitarian-assistance workers have a colossal job ahead of them.

"I've been doing relief work for 30 years," said Johns, of Catholic Relief Services, who has worked in Cambodia, Ethiopia, East Timor, Somalia, Rwanda, and Kosovo, among other places. "This is the worst devastation I've ever seen. The only thing I can compare it to are the images of Hiroshima after they droped the atomic bomb."

The World Food Program is bringing 240 tons of food a day into Banda Aceh by truck caravan from Medan, some 250 miles to the southeast, said Mike Huggins, the organization's local spokesman. The Australian military recently flew in 60 tons of high-energy biscuits.

In a fortuitous turn of events, the government of Japan donated 12,500 tons of rice that happened to be passing through the region en route to Bangladesh when the tsunami struck. They sent it to Banda Aceh instead.

A host of relief groups meet each day at the WFP headquarters—a tiny cinderblock building next to a tennis court—to decide where the food should go.

Until recently, when they received tents and cots, the staff here had been sleeping on a tennis court. About 50 people were sharing one bathroom and using buckets of water to bathe.

A caravan of trucks rumbles out of the nearby WFP warehouse each day and takes supplies to devastated villages and the dozens of refugee camps that have sprung up across the region.

Recently, they delivered a truckload of rice to a camp in Matayi, a Banda Aceh neighborhood where 3,500 people have taken up temporary residence on the grounds of a local television station.

A shed at the entrance is plastered with pictures of people who disappeared in the tsunami, hung there by relatives still hoping to find them.

Many of the people helping run the camp are victims of the tsunami themselves. They have developed a food-distribution system under which they have divided the camp into 150 groups of about 30 people. Each group receives a ration of rice, biscuits, noodles, cooking oil and milk each day.

The diet is monotonous, but the refugees said there is enough food.

Among the people waiting for something to eat on was

(above) Tsunami-stricken Aceh, Sumatra island, Indonesia Thursday Jan. 5, 2005. (right) An aerial shot taken from a helicopter shows boats stranded on the shore after the powerful tidal wave in the coastal town Galle, Sri Lanka.

Hasan Basri, 43, and his wife, Qunuti, 39. They come from a Banda Aceh suburb called Peukun Bada, which was leveled by the tsunami.

Basri, Qunuti and their 10-year-old daughter survived, but virtually everyone else on both sides of their extended family—some 40 people in all—disappeared.

Basri teaches accounting at a local university that was wiped out. "I have nothing left," he said. "I came here to find food."

His English was so good that Huggins of the WFP decided to hire him on the spot to help with the relief effort.

"This the world's worst natural disaster," Huggins said. "No one has dealt with a crisis like this before." ▪